Brown, Gene.

Conflict in Europe
and the Great
Depression.

$15.98

DATE			

BAKER & TAYLOR

First Person
A★M★E★R★I★C★A

CONFLICT IN EUROPE
—— AND ——
THE GREAT DEPRESSION

World War I (1914–1940)

Gene Brown

Twenty-First Century Books

A Division of Henry Holt and Company
New York

Twenty-First Century Books
A Division of Henry Holt and Company, Inc.
115 West 18th Street
New York, New York 10011

Henry Holt® and colophon are trademarks of Henry Holt and
Company, Inc.
Publishers since 1866

©1993 by Blackbirch Graphics, Inc.
First Edition
5 4 3 2 1

Published in Canada by Fitzhenry & Whiteside Ltd.
195 Allstate Parkway, Markham, Ontario L3R 4T8

Printed in the United States of America
All first editions are printed on acid-free paper ∞.

Created and produced in association with Blackbirch Graphics, Inc.

Library of Congress Cataloging-in-Publication Data

Brown, Gene.
    Conflict in Europe and the Great Depression: World War I (1914–1940) /
Gene Brown.
        p.   cm. — (First person America)
    Includes index.
    ISBN 0-8050-2585-5
    1. United States—History—20th century—Sources—Juvenile literature.
2. History, Modern—20th century—Sources—Juvenile literature.   I. Title.
II. Series.
E741.B74 1993
973.9—dc20
                                                                    93-24998
                                                                        CIP
                                                                        AC

CONTENTS

Private P. Loughlin of the U.S. Army bids his family farewell before he joins the battle in Europe in 1917 (*National Archives*).

INTRODUCTION

It was between the beginning of World War I and the eve of World War II that modern America was born. American society went through major changes, not only in politics and economics, but also in the way people led their daily lives.

The Americans who elected Woodrow Wilson still thought of themselves as distant from their quarreling neighbors in Europe. And when U.S. soldiers were sent to France to fight in World War I, most Americans saw it merely as a temporary change in foreign policy. The troops would come home when the fighting stopped, many believed, and life would go back to normal.

The country that the soldiers returned to was just reaching the point where more people lived in cities than in rural areas. Statistically, people who lived in the country were just as likely not to have electricity as have it, and indoor plumbing was for many still a luxury. Washing machines and vacuum cleaners had still not appeared in large numbers, even in big cities.

When it came time to relax, Americans were more likely to play ball than go to a ballpark to watch a game. They were also more likely to play an instrument—especially a piano—or sing in groups, than listen to records. The phonograph, however, was rapidly becoming popular. Feature-length movies were new, as was the practice of following the careers and lives of particular "stars."

The federal government, much smaller and with less control over daily life than it has now, seemed distant. Without radio or TV, it still took a long time to find out what was going on in Washington.

By the second decade of the 1900s, there were already some protests about racial prejudice, but if polls had existed—which they didn't—they probably would have shown that most Americans thought blacks were not the social equals of whites. Sentiment was strong, however, to give women the right to vote—and by 1920, they would have it. In some areas, such as New York City's Greenwich Village, certain women were even talking about gaining equal rights in all aspects of society, but they were an exception. Voting rights might be acceptable, but most of the country still thought that women belonged in the kitchen.

While the rise of organized crime and political corruption of the 1920s had hurt the reputation of politicians and businessmen, they were still largely respected.

Twenty years later, by the late 1930s, America had survived a terrible economic depression brought on, to a large extent, by the crash of the stock market in 1929. To fight these terrible problems, the size of the federal government had been increased enormously, now affecting almost every aspect of daily life. Among other things, a national police force, the Federal Bureau of Investigation (F.B.I.), had been set up to deal with people plotting against the government as well as gangsters who took advantage of Prohibition (legal ban on alcohol).

Unions, strong in only a few industries at the time of World War I, were fast reaching a peak of power in the 1930s. One change they were bringing about in many industries was the 40-hour work week, a change that firmly established the now cherished two-day weekend for the first time.

By the late 1930s, protests against racial prejudice were becoming more frequent. The majority of women in the United States were still in the home, although more of them were beginning to work at outside jobs. In a few years, World War II would give many more women a major opportunity to get out of the house and earn a paycheck.

Abroad, America's isolationist foreign policy was about to end. Now, there would be no turning back from seizing a new role in global leadership. As it headed toward yet another world war in the early 1940s, the United States would be the greatest economic and military power on the planet, a far cry from that earlier America of World War I that sent soldiers "over there."

Men stand in line at a soup kitchen in Washington, D.C. during the Depression (*National Archives*).

CHAPTER 1

FIGHTING A WAR IN EUROPE

Peace Without Victory

B y the second decade of the twentieth century, the economic power of the United States was becoming a global force. Had such a powerful country been located in Europe, its industrial might would have greatly influenced the foreign policy of every other country nearby. But the United States was not nearby. A great ocean separated America from Europe's political conflicts.

Since its birth as a nation, the United States had mostly followed a policy of "isolation." It tried not to get involved at all in the affairs of Europe, and, in turn, it expected Europe to stay out of America's business.

But now there were forces at work that would change all this. The development of large and powerful navies had made the Atlantic much less of an obstacle to cross. Germany's navy, especially, had become a threat to America's shipping industry. Isolationism was no longer working for America and it was being inevitably drawn closer to the war that had been raging in Europe since 1914.

Knowing America had to play a role abroad, the country's leaders were faced with defining exactly what that role would be. Many advocated victory at any cost for America's allies—and for itself, if it was pulled into the fighting. Most Americans thought the enemy should be crushed without mercy. But President Woodrow Wilson (1856-1924) had other ideas. He thought this approach would simply lay the groundwork for the next war, and the next. Wilson wanted America to stand for something more, something better than the "power politics" or "balance of power" that seemed to guide the statesmen of Europe.

President Wilson addresses the Congress in 1917 (*National Archives*).

The Treaty of Versailles, signed in 1919, formally marked the end of World War I (*National Portrait Gallery*).

"Power politics" meant that a nation's foreign policy was based solely on strength. A large arms industry and numerous armed forces could make a country powerful, and alliances with other countries could make it even more powerful.

"Balance of power" was the idea that groups of allies, if of relatively equal strength, would keep war from breaking out. Members of alliances would feel protected from attack and would not try to upset the balance because all other nations had their allies, too. In fact, the balance did not work, as the outbreak of World War I had shown.

Woodrow Wilson, as the president of a nation founded on ideals, wanted a foreign policy with higher aims. In the speech that follows, he calls for the settling of international conflicts on the basis of fairness and justice, not just strength.

Many ridiculed the president as unrealistic for calling for "peace without victory." After the war, at the peace conference in Versailles, Europe's statesmen drew up a treaty based on the usual power politics and the balance of power. They did, however, agree to a League of Nations that would try to settle international disputes peacefully, with justice.

Unfortunately for President Wilson, when the war ended, isolationism became popular once again in America and the U.S. Congress voted against joining the League of Nations. It would be another twenty-five years, and take another world war, before America and the world finally made Wilson's ideas a reality. Today, the United Nations organization headquarters stands in New York City as a tribute to the ideals Wilson had in mind when he delivered the following speech.

Wilson Speaks to the Senate—January 22, 1917

No covenant of co-operative peace that does not include the peoples of the New World can suffice to keep the future safe against war; and yet there is only one sort of peace that the peoples of America could join in guaranteeing. The elements of that peace must be elements that engage the confidence and satisfy the principles of the American governments.

It will be absolutely necessary that a force be created as a guarantor of the permanency of the settlement so much greater than the force of any nation now engaged or any alliance hitherto formed or projected that no nation, no probable combination of nations could face or withstand it. If the peace presently to be made is to endure, it must be a peace made secure by the organized major force of mankind.

The question upon which the whole future peace and policy of the world depends is this: Is the present war a struggle for a just and secure peace, or only for a new balance of power? If it be only a struggle for a new balance of power, who will guarantee, who *can* guarantee the stable equilibrium of the new arrangement? Only a tranquil Europe can be a stable Europe. There must be, not a balance of power, but a community of power; not organized rivalries, but an organized common peace.

It must be a peace without victory.

Victory would mean peace forced upon the loser, a victor's terms imposed upon the vanquished. It would be accepted in humiliation, under duress, at an intolerable sacrifice, and would leave a sting, a resentment, a bitter memory upon which terms of peace would rest, not permanently, but only as upon quicksand. Only a peace between equals can last. Only a peace the very principle of which is equality and a common participation in a common benefit. The right state of mind, the right feeling between nations, is as necessary for a lasting peace as is the just settlement of vexed questions of territory or of racial and national allegiance.

The equality of nations upon which peace must be founded if it is to last must be an equality of rights; the guarantees exchanged must neither recognize nor imply a difference between big nations and small, between those that are powerful and those that are weak.

From: *Documents of American History,* by Henry Steele Commager. "Peace Without Victory" Address of President Wilson, January 22, 1917 (New York: Appleton-Century-Crofts, 1968).

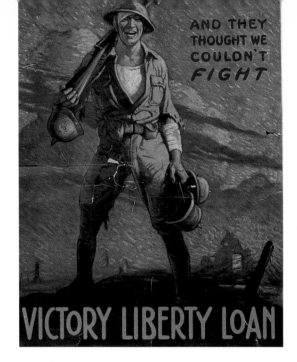

AND THEY THOUGHT WE COULDN'T *FIGHT*

VICTORY LIBERTY LOAN

A World War I propaganda poster reminds Americans to invest money in order to help the war effort (*National Archives*).

The Usefulness of Propaganda

When the United States entered World War I in 1917, it knew that it would need to use all its resources to bring its allies to victory. The United States had a total of eleven allies. The allied group was made up of the following countries: Russia, France, Great Britain, Italy, Japan, Rumania, Serbia, Belgium, Greece, Portugal, and Montenegro. The idea of mobilizing the entire United States for a war had begun about a half-century before, in the Civil War. The Civil War broke new ground because the entire civilian population on each side—not just some paid soldiers, or mercenaries—played a part. A military draft, for example, turned much of the adult male population into soldiers.

By 1917, new methods of mass communication made it possible to rally the entire American population—newspapers and radio broadcasts could get the country to focus its hate on the "enemy" and to work hard doing whatever it could to win the war. With the rise of this mass media, and the propaganda it could create, ideas quickly became effective weapons.

One important tool of propaganda was the mass production of cheap newspapers, able to print vivid pictures that could stir hundreds of thousands of people at once and sway public opinion. Another tool was the movies, barely twenty years old but already a powerful force for shaping the way people saw the world.

Today we take for granted that the media—including radio and television—are important in influencing public opinion. But in 1917, this idea was still new. Using newspapers, movies, and other kinds of communication to influence public opinion opened up a whole new frontier for politicians and other important social leaders.

On April 14, 1917, President Wilson set up a Committee on Public Information (CPI) that would be responsible for getting the government's message to the people and getting the people behind the government. Journalist Edward Bernays worked with this group, and, in the following excerpt, gives a brief account of the work he did.

While the committee disbanded when the war ended, the methods they developed for influencing public opinion were just beginning. Not only would government continue to use these methods, business and other institutions would, too. In fact, Edward Bernays is often said to have invented this new field, now called public relations.

Edward Bernays (*Wide World Photos*)

Edward Bernays on Influencing the Public

The Foreign Press Bureau of the committee, initiated in November 1917, supplemented the cable and wireless news sent to overseas media by the press services and the CPI. It supplied interpretation and background material that emphasized America's contribution to the war effort. It was seven months old and growing fast when I started working with it. The CPI was constructed overnight and in the face of bitter and continuous attack from Republicans and others who feared the potential power of a Government propaganda agency.

We sent articles, photographs, cuts and mats on American agriculture, labor, religion, medicine and education to overseas posts for placement and to American trade publications that had circulation in foreign countries; our material always stressed Woodrow Wilson's ideals and the good will of the American people toward other peoples. We staged events in the U.S. that dramatized our propaganda themes. We distributed statements made by the President, the Secretary of State and other officials and newsworthy private citizens. And when unfavorable news came from the front, we tried to counteract it with stories on our war effort.

From: *Biography of an Idea: Memoirs of the Public Relations Counsel* by Edward L. Bernays (New York: Simon & Schuster, 1965). Reprinted by permission.

Whose War?

In 1981, Warren Beatty directed and starred in a movie called *Reds*. Winner of three Academy Awards, it was the story of John Reed (1887-1920), a young American radical who went to Russia when the Communists staged their revolution in 1917. Reed wrote about what he saw in his now famous book, *Ten Days That Shook The World*, still considered one of the best first-hand accounts of the Russian Revolution.

A journalist, Reed was an editor of the radical magazine, *The Masses*, and one of the founders of the American Communist Party. *The Masses* did not attempt to be objective, as you will see in the following selection. It had a strong point of view. The journal was on the side of the poor against the rich, the workers against the bosses. As one of the editors, Reed wanted to mobilize American public opinion. He wanted to show why the government's effort to get the country behind the war in Europe would hurt America. He said that fighting in World War I would destroy civil liberties.

The Espionage Act of 1917 and the Sedition Act of 1918 allowed the government to round up and deport people on evidence that, by today's standards, most would consider skimpy. These acts also provided for censorship of speech and written material that was seen as "subversive" or against the popular good. Reed's magazine, *The Masses*, was quickly identified by the government as subversive, and was shut down.

There are, of course, other issues concerning free speech during war time. What are the limits, if any, to free speech when the country is at war? This is a question that is still debated today.

Right or wrong, John Reed stood up for a point of view about which he felt passionate. Even though the government quickly silenced him, he raised his voice on the issue of security versus freedom when America was hearing almost nothing but support for joining the battle in World War I.

John Reed, at work in his office (*Culver Pictures*).

John Reed Warns America

I know what war means. I have been with the armies of all the belligerents except one, and I have seen men die, and go mad, and lie in hospitals suffering hell; but there is a worse thing than that. War means an ugly mob-madness, crucifying the truth-tellers, choking the artists, side-tracking reforms, revolutions, and the working of social forces. Already in America those citizens who oppose the entrance of their country into the European melée are called "traitors," and those who protest against the curtailing of our meagre rights of free speech are spoken of as "dangerous lunatics." . . . . The press is howling for war. The church is howling for war. Lawyers, politicians, stock-brokers, social leaders are all howling for war.

Whose war is this? Not mine. I know that hundreds of thousands of American workingmen employed by our great financial "patriots" are not paid a living wage. I have seen poor men sent to jail for long terms without trial, and even without any charge. Peaceful strikers, and their wives and children, have been shot to death, burned to death, by private detectives and militiamen. The rich have steadily become richer, and the cost of living higher, and the workers proportionally poorer. These toilers don't want war—not even civil war. But the speculators, the employers, the plutocracy—they want it, just as they did in Germany and in England; and with lies and sophistries they will whip up our blood until we are savage—and then we'll fight and die for them.

From: "Whose War?" *The Masses*, April, 1917. From William L. O'Neill, ed. *Echoes of Revolt: The Masses*, 1911-1917 (New York: Quadrangle Books, 1966). Reprinted by permission.

CHAPTER 2

THE ERA OF
"RUGGED INDIVIDUALISM"

How Much Government Is Too Much?

Today the government is so involved in the running of our society that it's hard to imagine life without programs such as unemployment insurance, Medicare, and Social Security. Americans have grown dependent upon these programs and would suffer greatly if they were eliminated entirely. Yet, before the presidency of Franklin Roosevelt and his New Deal of the 1930s, people were mostly on their own when coping with hard times. If natural or human-made disaster struck, charity or help from friends and family was the only resort.

Herbert Hoover (1874-1964), the last president before the great New Deal expansion of government, was a spokesman for the view that said people who relied on no one but themselves were those who had made this country strong. In the selection that follows, he blames the government in Washington for growing too large and getting into people's business too much during World War I. He saw this kind of government interference as a disaster.

In 1928, shortly after he made the remarks that follow in the next excerpt, Hoover was elected president. A year later the stock market crashed and American business soon came to a standstill. People lost their jobs, and suffered without any help from the government—there wasn't any unemployment insurance back then. Many Americans also lost their life savings when a number of major banks failed. As banks foreclosed on mortgages, some people were forced to build shacks from wood scraps, tar paper, and other discarded material for shelter. Groups of shacks could often be seen in public parks and on empty lots. These little "cities" were commonly called "Hoovervilles."

President Hoover tried to have government do something for failing businesses. He set up the Reconstruction Finance Corporation, but his overriding belief that government should leave people alone kept him from acting further.

Democratic administrations in the 1930s and later would popularize the idea of government doing those things that individuals could not do for themselves. Eventually, however, there was a popular reaction against strong government intervention. Voters in the 1980s, by electing presidents Reagan and Bush, swung back toward Hoover's idea that most responsibility

Herbert Hoover, portrait by American painter Douglas Chandor (*National Portrait Gallery*).

should be left to individuals. Then, when the economy stumbled badly in the late 1980s, Americans changed course and went back to the Democratic approach by electing Bill Clinton in 1992.

What is the correct amount of government intervention for the American economy? That's still a matter about which people strongly disagree. The debate begins in 1928, with Herbert Hoover.

Hoover Promotes Government Without Intervention

When the war closed, the most vital of all issues both in our own country and throughout the world was whether governments should continue their wartime ownership and operation of many instru-mentalities of production and distribution. We were challenged with a peace-time choice between the American system of rugged individualism and a European philosophy of diametrically opposed doctrines—doctrines of paternalism self-government through centralization of government. It would have meant the undermining of the individual initiative and enterprise through which our people have grown to unparalleled greatness.

When the Republican Party came into full power it went at once resolutely back to our funda-mental conception of the state and the rights and responsibilities of the individual. Thereby it restored confidence and hope in the American people, it freed and stimulated enterprise, it restored the gov-ernment to its position as an umpire instead of a player in the economic game. For these reasons the American people have gone forward in progress while the rest of the world has halted, and some countries have even gone backwards.

From: "The Philosophy of Rugged Individualism." Speech by Herbert Hoover, New York City, October 22, 1928.

America's Economy in Ruins

Gordon Parks, age 16, (later to become a famous photographer) had to work after school in 1929 at a private club in St. Paul, Minnesota to make ends meet. In the excerpt that follows, he recalls the momentous day when the New York Stock Exchange crashed and the roof fell in on his world.

Parks lost his job, and many club members suddenly found themselves in financial trouble because of what happened in the stock market. For much of the 1920s, Wall Street had been a symbol of America's optimism. Now it would stand for the worst excesses of the nation's economy.

Herbert Hoover had said that "rugged individualism" was the key to the American way. He meant that people and the nation would grow wealthy through hard work if government did not interfere with their efforts. But many Americans wanted a shortcut. They wanted to make money fast, without the hard work, by investing in the "market."

Interest in the stock market spread like wildfire in the late 1920s. The market became as much a part of everyday talk as sports and the latest neighborhood gossip. Everyone, it seemed, knew someone who knew just which stocks to buy. These "hot tips," passed along as sure things, were really not more than hunches. People who would never have thought of investing began frantically buying shares. People thought if they didn't buy while the price was low, they would regret it when the price went up.

This frenzy of investment, called speculation, became feverish by the late 1920s. One economist, John Kenneth Galbraith, has called it "lunacy." The value of stocks kept going up because people were buying them on the hope that they would go up some more. The value of these shares began to have no connection to the success or failure of the companies that issued them.

What's worse, many people were buying stocks with borrowed money—called buying "on margin." People were safe as long as the value of their shares kept rising. Under "rugged individualism," the government did not regulate the market as it does today, so no one was able to slow things down when speculation got out of control.

For several days in late October 1929, the first major losses to stockholders appeared. Then, on Tuesday, October 29, total panic set in. It seemed that nearly everyone tried to pull out of the market at the same time. For some shares of stock, there were no buyers at any price. Optimism went up in smoke as fortunes disappeared within hours.

The stock market crash did not cause the Great Depression alone, but it helped to bring it on. Years would pass before the average American would trust his or her money to the market again.

Panicked investors gather outside near the New York Stock Exchange on October 29, 1929, the day of the "great crash" (*Wide World Photos*).

Gordon Parks Remembers the Crash

The employees' locker room at the club was unusually quiet when I arrived at work on Wednesday. Waiters who had known each other for years were sitting about as though they were strangers. The cause of the silence was tacked to the bulletin board. It read: "Because of unforeseen circumstances, some personnel will be laid off the first of next month. Those directly affected will be notified in due time. The management."

"That Hoover's ruining the country," an old waiter finally said. No one answered him. I changed into my suit of blue tails, wondering what had happened.

By Thursday the entire world knew. "MARKET CRASHES—PANIC HITS NATION!" one headline blared. The newspapers were full of it, and I read everything I could get my hands on, gathering in the full meaning of such terms as Black Thursday, deflation and depression. I couldn't imagine such financial disaster touching my small world; it surely concerned only the rich. But by the first week of November I too knew differently; along with millions of others across the nation, I was without a job. All that next week I searched for any kind of work that would prevent my leaving school. Again it was, "We're firing, not hiring." "Sorry, sonny, nothing doing here." Finally, on the seventh of November I went to school and cleaned out my locker, knowing it was impossible to stay on.

From: Milton Meltzer, *Brother Can You Spare a Dime? The Great Depression, 1929–1933* (New York: Harper & Row, 1969). Reprinted by permission.

CHAPTER 3

MODERN AMERICA EMERGES

The Growth of Rural America

If historians had to pick a decade in which America first began to resemble the country we live in today, many would probably choose the 1920s. The 1920 census showed that, for the first time, more people lived in urban than in rural areas. It also showed that enough people owned cars to justify the beginning of a vast nationwide system of roads and highways.

With radios starting to appear in many homes and the movies reaching great popularity, Americans were sharing some of the same entertainment no matter where they lived. In the stores, canned and frozen foods were just starting to replace fresh produce, and much of it carried a "brand name," such as Birds Eye.

William Allen White, editor of the *Emporia Gazette* in Kansas, was sensitive to many of these changes.

His *Autobiography* is an account of how the birth of modern America transformed his small city. In the following piece, he remembers an earlier time, when national interests, customs, fads, and food took second place to local concerns and activities. White also recalls when change came more gradually to Emporia. Now it seemed that everything changed so fast.

Along with America's cities, the size of the middle class was also growing. People had more money and could buy new products, such as household appliances and cars, which American factories were turning out rapidly. This, in turn, made for more jobs and the chance for even more people to join the middle class.

An Oregon farm family listens to a recently purchased radio in 1925. The growth of technology rapidly changed rural America during the 1920s (*National Archives*).

Small-town America wasn't always happy with all these changes. "Old-fashioned" values, such as thrift, for example, sometimes seemed threatened by the new idea of spending for today instead of saving for tomorrow. Nor was everybody comfortable with the way business, advertising, and salesmanship was now influencing everything from politics to food shopping.

A few years after the following piece was written, the Great Depression would temporarily put a stop to much of this change. But the foundations would still hold. And after World War II, the growth of cities, a mass-market economy, and the continued growth of mass media would become even more the story of America for the rest of the century.

William Allen White Remembers Emporia

Sallie and I came home in midspring of 1924 to Emporia, after three months abroad, to find the town in a building boom. The advertising patronage of the paper was growing rapidly, crowding extra pages in every day. A new linotype which we had bought in the previous year did not relieve the pressure in the composing room. Merchants were spending their money freely to attract buyers. And from the East, came thousands of dollars in advertising, calling attention to national products—automobiles, radios, phonographs, tobacco, oil, transportation—a long list of things which once were luxuries and were becoming the common comforts of the people. The economic revolution was going full tilt. A whole class was moving up in its standard of living, in its self-respect, in its attitude toward life. The serving class in America was passing. The machine was becoming the servant. The servant was joining the master class. New houses all over Emporia were replacing the old houses and the character of every street was changing.

Our first three-story, brick apartment building in the town was ready for occupancy—another sign, a social sign, that the economic revolution was achieving its purpose. The home was changing. Old America, the America of "our Fathers' pride," the America wherein a frugal people had grown great through thrift and industry, was disappearing before the new machine age. Mass production was accumulating and distributing wealth.

The miracle of the radio was becoming a commonplace in the humblest home. Kansas was presently to have enough automobiles to put every man, woman, and child in the state on wheels at the same time.

From: *The Autobiography of William Allen White* by William Allen White (New York: Macmillan, 1946). Reprinted by permission.

Problems with Prohibition

During the 1920s, Prohibition was called "The Great Experiment." For decades, many Americans, especially Protestants, had campaigned to ban the sale of alcoholic drinks. Parades, petitions, and political action had finally gotten results. With the end of World War I, the manufacture and sale of beer, wine, and liquor became illegal.

But as with the banning of drug use today, passing a law and making it work were not the same thing. Many Americans thought the law was foolish; they said it wouldn't work and would cause more harm than good. In the end, it seemed that they were right.

People did not stop drinking during Prohibition. But since it was sometimes hard to get the real thing, they often downed poorly made liquor that made them sick. As for the real thing, those who could afford alcohol could usually get it. Liquor was brought in illegally across the Canadian border or smuggled in on

An illegal still is shut down by Detroit police during Prohibition (*National Archives*).

ships. Or it came from homemade stills set up in basements and warehouses. Alcohol was also available in the back rooms of old bars, for steady customers. And it was found in "speakeasies," illegal bars and clubs where patrons had to give a password at the door in order to get in.

The most serious result of Prohibition was the social effect of all this illegal activity. When people are willing to spend enormous amounts of money on something—even if it is illegal—criminals will take advantage of it and find the easiest ways to provide it.

In the 1920s, Al Capone (1899-1947) was an expert at this. Born in New York, he rose to fame in Chicago as a "bootlegger," making a living from the illegal manufacture, transportation, and sale of alcohol.

Al Capone (left) talks with his attorney, Albert Fink during a federal trial for tax evasion (*Wide World Photos*).

Capone ran his operation like a business. To run it smoothly, he bribed police and public officials to "look the other way," spreading and encouraging corruption on a massive scale. As the following remembrance by Chicago journalist Edward Dean Sullivan points out, Capone was called "Mr. Capone" at City Hall. He also helped otherwise law-abiding citizens get used to the idea of regularly breaking the law.

By the time the Depression took hold in the early 1930s, Americans voted Prohibition out. Al Capone's legacy was the gang he left behind and the idea that the methods of big business could be used to break the law through "organized" crime. Today, organized crime continues to plague our society on many levels, threatening the safety and well-being of us all.

On the Mind of Al Capone

As a newspaper man I have known Al Capone for eight years.

I know what he was, what prohibition made him, and I know what his ingenuity, hard work, and topsy-turvy success means as an example to the very worst element in this country.

Al Capone, better known as "Scarface," is the head of one gang of the more than eight hundred powerful gangs now at work in this country under prohibition. In 1926 the gross income of his one gang was seventy million dollars.

Listen to him:

"Prohibition is a business. All I do is to supply a public demand. I do it in the best and least harmful way I can.

"I can't change conditions. I just meet them without backing up.

"Most of my business is in Chicago. When prohibition came in there were seven thousand five hundred saloons there. Chicago spent nearly a hundred million dollars for booze at the old prices. Nobody wanted prohibition. Chicago voted six to one against it. Somebody had to throw some liquor on that thirst. Why not me?

"My customers include some of the finest people in the city, or in the world, for that matter. But I am just a bootlegger. I violate the prohibition law. All right—so do they!"

In the ten years of Al Capone's reign in Chicago there have been 4,000 homicides. At least half of them have had some relation to booze, gang, and racketeer activity. For every thirty men in these branches of twisted industry and slaughter there is one "Big Shot" or leader. Seventy Big Shots have been killed since 1924 in Chicago, and the only one who was nearly convicted was James J. Doherty, political gangster. The state's attorney who prosecuted him and failed to convict him, after what was assumed to be a most brilliant effort in prosecution, was subsequently found dead next to the gangster defendant after a gang battle at Cicero. They were making their twentieth visit together at a saloon which was a pay-off spot for the gangsters.

Al Capone is usually indicted for any murder in Cicero, and he was indicted in this case. Four months later, in his own good time, he gave himself up—to have it over with. He was freed of the charge.

From: *The Liberty Years, 1924–1950*, Churchill, ed. (Englewood, NJ: Prentice-Hall, 1969). Reprinted by permission.

A New Black Nationalism

Langston Hughes
(*National Portrait Gallery*).

For many African Americans, the new middle-class America was something that seemed forever out of reach. The cruelty of racism allowed few blacks to get the kinds of jobs that allowed them to give their children a better life than they had lived. They also faced discrimination of a more personal kind. In the South, they were officially segregated (separated by race). Although racism was usually less spelled out in the North, it was almost as bad. For example, the law might not say where they could not live, but real estate companies "restricted" certain areas, refusing to rent or sell to blacks.

How could African Americans ever expect to live in dignity? While organizations such as the National Association for the Advancement of Colored People (NAACP) pushed to get white America to accept black citizens as equals, another approach gained supporters in the 1920s. This was black nationalism.

This decade saw the formation of large black neighborhoods in Northern cities, to which people had moved from rural areas in the South. The most famous of these was New York's Harlem, which was fast becoming the cultural capital of black America. Here jazz, rooted in the South, was taking on a more urban form through brilliant musicians such as Duke Ellington (1899-1974), Louis Armstrong (1900-1971), and Fats Waller (1904-1943). Black authors such as Langston Hughes (1902-1967) were starting to make major contributions to American literature and many prominent members of black society were influencing and creating the new "style" of the 1920s and 1930s.

In Harlem lived a black man, born in the West Indies, who took seriously the expression "Why don't you go back where you came from?" He thought this was a good idea—the only one that would really work for African Americans. He supported a mass return by all blacks in America to Africa, the "motherland."

Marcus Garvey (1887-1940) formed his Universal Negro Improvement Association in 1914. He had a two-part program. Garvey said that rather than trying to mix with whites who didn't want them, blacks should have their own country. He also called for a separate existence for blacks within white America. African Americans, he said, should have their own businesses and shop only in places owned by other blacks. Garvey's organization opened many businesses so that blacks could buy from fellow blacks.

Marcus Garvey travels through Harlem in the uniform he adopted as the President of the Republic of Africa (*Wide World Photos*).

In the 1920s, Garvey was probably the most prominent opponent of the NAACP's goal of integration into white society. He encouraged black pride with parades and other activities. Here was the first strong statement of the black nationalism that would be heard forty years later, in the 1960s.

Marcus Garvey, Against Integration

There is but one solution, and that is to provide an outlet for Negro energy, ambition, and passion, away from the attraction of white opportunity and surround the race with opportunities of its own. If this is not done, and if the foundation for same is not laid now, then the consequences will be sorrowful for the weaker race, and be disgraceful to white ideals of justice, and shocking to white civilization.

The Negro must have a country, and a nation of his own. If you laugh at the idea, then you are selfish and wicked, for you and your children do not intend that the Negro shall discommode you in yours. If you do not want him to have a country and a nation of his own; if you do not intend to give him equal opportunities in yours; then it is plain to see that you mean that he must die even as the Indian to make room for another race.

Let the Negroes have a Government of their own. Don't encourage them to believe that they will become social equals and leaders of the whites in America, without first on their own account proving to the world that they are capable of evolving a civilization of their own. The white race can best help the Negro by telling him the truth, and not by flattering him into believing that he is as good as any white man without first proving the racial, national constructive metal of which he is made.

Stop flattering the Negro about social equality, and tell him to go to work and build for himself. Help him in the direction of doing for himself, and let him know that self progress brings its own reward.

From: 1924 Pamphlet—Marcus Garvey, "An Appeal to the Soul of White America." United Negro Improvement Association.

CHAPTER 4

THE GROWTH OF MASS MEDIA AND MASS CULTURE

Movies Become an American Industry

Today, famous movie stars are usually in control of their careers. They know that their name on a film can often mean millions of extra tickets sold. The movie companies know it as well. But this wasn't always the case.

By the mid-1920s, the movies—which were silent then—were wildly popular. Along with cheap newspapers and radio, they were the beginning of what today is called the mass media. The ideas and values expressed in films, even the fashions worn in them, reached into every corner of America and touched the lives of nearly everyone. There was almost no sizeable town that didn't have at least one movie house. The big cities had many, some of which were called "palaces" because they were so fancy.

The movies were very much a business, with facilities for producing, distributing, advertising, and retailing their product. The movies' stars were an important part of this product. Stardom on a national scale was a new thing. Live theater produced some famous names, but almost none got the attention that movie fan magazines paid to movie actors.

These stars were not just professional actors. They were "personalities" and celebrities, such as Mary Pickford (1893-1979), Douglas Fairbanks (1883-1939), and Lillian Gish (1893-1993). People wanted to know every detail of their lives. When few facts were available, fans imagined the rest.

Lillian Gish (*Photofest*).

The men who ran the movie studios knew how important this idea of stardom was. If there was not enough interesting information about the private life of a star, they might feel it necessary to "create" something, such as the "scandal" mentioned in the following selection. Scandal led to publicity and publicity meant more sales at the box office. Here were many of the public relations techniques developed by Edward Bernays in action.

The following account describes Lillian Gish's dealings with MGM executives. At the time, Irving Thalberg (1899-1936) was chief of production at the studio, and "Mr. Mayer" was Louis B. Mayer (1885-1957), vice-president and head of MGM. David W. Griffith (1875–1948), "Mr. Griffith," was a movie director and worked with Lillian Gish.

Lillian Gish: A Screen Star Remembers

During my talks with Irving Thalberg over *Anna Karenina* I was suddenly sent for by Mr. Mayer, who had some papers for me to sign. I explained that I had promised my lawyer not to sign anything without his approval. Mr. Mayer grew angry and said I ought to trust him. He explained that he wanted to take me off salary until they had a story ready for me. I had gone off salary while I was in England, but since then there had been ample time for them to prepare a script for me.

"If you don't do as I say, I can ruin you," Mr. Mayer said.

It was the second time I had heard that threat. "I'm sure you can, but I gave my word," I said. "I can't break that; else how could you or anyone else ever trust me again?"

Irving spoke to me about renewing my contract. "We would like to have you stay with us," he said, "but there is something we think would be wise to do."

I knew Irving was my friend, so I listened.

"You see, you are way up there on a pedestal," he explained, "and nobody cares. If you were knocked off the pedestal, everyone would care." He added earnestly, "Let me arrange a scandal for you."

I was startled. The irony of the suggestion made me want to laugh.

What kind of scandal did Irving want to arrange? I wondered. A romantic scandal, I decided—but for what? To sell pictures? Had the public changed so much? All my life I had been taught to keep my name clean. Mr. Griffith had always maintained that one touch of scandal would finish you in pictures. What had happened to change this? And, after the scandal had died down, they would be obliged to dream up another. Could I be on stage constantly—with a prearranged scandal before the release of each new picture?

My answer was a decisive *No*.

I told Irving my decision, knowing that my days at M.G.M. were numbered.

From: Lillian Gish (with Ann Pinchot), *The Movies: Mr. Griffith and Me.* (Englewood, NJ: Prentice-Hall, 1969). Reprinted by permission.

America's Favorite Pastime Emerges

T he following selection, by a baseball player from "the old school," is about a time before there were free agents, multiyear contracts, and vast sums of money paid to athletes who endorsed products. It's also about baseball before television.

Professional baseball on a large scale dates from the turn of the century. The growth of cities and of spare time from work—most important, the creation of the "weekend"—led to the development of many popular pastimes, including baseball. By the 1920s, there were also enough people with time and money to spend at the ballpark, which was now likely to be a large stadium rather than a small field.

Gradually, heroic figures developed in the sport. Christy Mathewson (1880-1925), Grover Cleveland Alexander (1887-1950), and Ty Cobb (1886-1961) were popular baseball icons. By the 1920s, some sports celebrities were becoming as big as movie stars. Perhaps the biggest of all was the New York Yankees' Babe Ruth (1895-1948). Everyone knew about him. He was world famous.

Lefty O'Doul, a major league ballplayer speaking in the following excerpt written in the 1960s, talks about America's favorite pastime and reminds us that organized sports as we know it today was not always such big corporate business. He also points out that scandal and improper behavior in professional sports are nothing new.

George Herman "Babe" Ruth (*National Portrait Gallery*).

Lefty O'Doul on Baseball

If I had it to do all over I'd be a ballplayer again without pay. Yeah, without pay. I loved it. That's why I never squawked when I didn't get big salaries. I liked to play too much.

Of course, if I were playing now and they gave some kid one of those big bonuses to sign a contract, why I'd be kind of disappointed in the whole setup. I led the National League in batting in 1929 with a .398 average, got 254 hits that season—still the record—and I got a $500 raise. That's right, $500.

Was I making about $20,000 then? Are you kidding? I was lucky to get as much as eight. In 1932 I led the National League in hitting again, with .368, and they *cut* me a thousand dollars. That's the truth!

How can they give these kids, without knowing what's inside their bodies, what kind of heart they have, what kind of intestinal fortitude, give them $100,000 to sign a contract? I can't understand it. Imagine if the Bank of America here would go to say Stanford University, and give the honor student there $100,000. And tell him that some day he'll be one of the big shots in the bank. Same idea. They wouldn't dare do that, would they?

When a man proves himself, has shown that he's a Big Leaguer, why I think those are the fellows should get the dough. Not some youngster who doesn't know his way into the ball park yet. I can't understand it. It doesn't help morale on a ball club, I'll tell you that.

From: *The Glory of Their Times*, Lawrence S. Ritter, ed. (New York: William Morrow, 1966, 1984). Reprinted by permission.

The Painful Sting of Discrimination

As popular as African-American entertainers were, discrimination was a fact of life for them in America. From the time that blacks became prominent in show business, they often had to perform in places that allowed only white people in the audience or on the dance floor. If the performance was at a hotel, the black entertainer was expected to enter from the service entrance, go on and do the show, and then find somewhere else to sleep that night.

This situation was well known in Harlem in the 1920s among African-American musicians and dancers. Suddenly, black culture was "in" and Harlem, or "uptown," was the place to go for knowledgeable white jazz fans at the time.

The most famous place in America to hear jazz was at Harlem's Cotton Club, where whites could pay $1.50 for dinner and see dancing great Bill "Bojangles" Robinson (1878-1949) or Duke Ellington and his orchestra. Owned by white gangsters, the Cotton Club was a showcase for some of the best black entertainers in the world. The ban on black customers did not affect every African American. A few could get in if they were famous, because whites did not object to sharing space with them.

Singer and band leader Cab Calloway (1907–   ), who played at the Cotton Club, remembered a stage surrounded by scenery that suggested a slave cabin on a cotton plantation in the South before the Civil War. "I suppose the idea was to make whites who came to the

club feel like they were being catered to and entertained by black slaves," he later wrote.

During World War II, at least one African-American entertainer decided that she just wouldn't tolerate racial discrimination anymore. Singer Lena Horne (1917–   ), performing at an army base in Arkansas, realized that along with white American soldiers, German prisoners of war were allowed in to hear her. But African-American soldiers were not. She walked out and refused to perform and her action stirred much controversy.

In the following excerpt, Herb Jeffries—a singer who performed with Duke Ellington—describes what life was like for black entertainers in the 1920s and 1930s. He specifically recalls the anger and humiliation he felt at seeing how fellow African Americans were treated throughout the United States.

Admired But Not Equal

When I joined Earl Hines in Chicago, in 1936, the racial situation was terrible. When we played one-nighters throughout the South, in places like Jacksonville, Florida, I can remember vividly how blacks were roped off. They could come in and listen to the band, but they couldn't dance. Only white people could dance. The blacks would stand off in a corner behind a big rope and listen.

The bandleaders all fought it. I was in Moline, Illinois, with Duke Ellington's band that had just come back from Europe where it had played for the royal family. And of course the Prince of Wales had sat in, you know, and played drums. But in Moline, blacks couldn't go to the restaurants to eat. Still, when anyone came backstage, the musicians would be finishing a show and people would be standing in line for autographs.

I don't think anybody was thrilled about the conditions, but if you wanted to advance and develop you couldn't show anger. You had to accept it and resign yourself to it. Little by little, blacks started saying, "If I can't live in this hotel, I won't play this hotel."

From: Joe Smith (Mitchell Fink, ed.), *Off The Record: An Oral History of Popular Music.* (New York: Warner Books, 1988). Reprinted by permission.

CHAPTER 5

A NEW DEAL FOR DARK TIMES

FDR Calms a Panicked Country

The excerpt that follows is from one of the most famous speeches in American history. In it, Franklin D. Roosevelt (1882-1945) had one chief aim: to stop the feeling of panic that gripped most of the country.

Roosevelt was taking office at a terrible time. Not only had the economy collapsed, people's faith in the "American Dream" had disappeared, too. Suddenly, there seemed to be no hope. Everything that people had been brought up to believe about the promise of America was being questioned.

Unemployment, for example, was headed toward 25 percent. (Today, 6 percent is considered very high.) Not only were almost one out of every four people out of work, there was no unemployment insurance to help the jobless. Those who still worked feared they would lose the jobs they had.

Afraid that the banks would collapse, people went to them in large numbers to withdraw all their money—this was known as a "run" on the bank. But this nationwide run actually caused the one thing people feared the most: bank failures. No bank kept enough money on hand to pay all depositors if they showed up at the same time. And unlike today, the government did not insure deposits. When banks failed, or ran out of cash, anyone who had money in them was out of luck.

With life savings wiped out in a single day, hundreds of thousands of Americans faced poverty. America did not yet have Social Security checks for retired people. Those who could no longer work had to live off their savings, or live with their children.

With the price of farm crops dropping and small businesses failing, farmers and businesspeople couldn't repay loans. This meant that many lost their farms and businesses, leaving them with nothing. These failures also brought down more banks, which now could not collect the money they had lent.

With each day seeming worse than the last, Roosevelt knew that he would have to stop this epidemic of hopelessness before specific measures could be taken to help the nation get back on its feet. So he used his first speech as president to remind the country that the people, along with their government, were not helpless and that they had the skills and the resources to turn things around. But they would have to "act," not just moan about how bad things were.

For his part, Roosevelt would, indeed, act. First, he declared a "bank holiday," a temporary breather to let the sense of panic die down. Then, in the next 100

days, he sent a host of new programs to Congress and got them passed in record time. They involved the government in the economy far more than it had ever been before.

To this day, people still disagree about FDR's "New Deal," as these programs came to be called. Some people feel that the New Deal was the first step toward an oversized and interfering government that controls too much of society. But whatever the New Deal's legacy might have been, Roosevelt did achieve his first aim. As president, he successfully calmed the "fear" that was paralyzing the country and preventing Americans from acting.

Franklin Delano Roosevelt addresses the nation at his inauguration in 1933 (*Wide World Photos*).

"The Only Thing We Have to Fear Is Fear Itself"

So first of all let me assert my firm belief that the only thing we have to fear is fear itself—nameless, unreasoning, unjustified terror which paralyzes needed efforts to convert retreat into advance.

Values have shrunken to fantastic levels; taxes have risen; our ability to pay has fallen, government of all kinds is faced by serious curtailment of income; the means of exchange are frozen in the currents of trade; the withered leaves of industrial enterprise lie on every side; farmers find no markets for their produce; the savings of many years in thousands of families are gone.

More important, a host of unemployed citizens face the grim problem of existence, and an equally great number toil with little return. Only a foolish optimist can deny the dark realities of the moment.

Our greatest primary task is to put people to work. This is no unsolvable problem if we face it wisely and courageously.

It can be accomplished in part by direct recruiting by the government itself, treating the task as we would treat the emergency of a war, but at the same time, through this employment, accomplishing greatly needed projects to stimulate and reorganize the use of our natural resources.

Hand in hand with this, we must frankly recognize the overbalance of population in our industrial centers and, by engaging on a national scale in the redistribution, endeavor to provide a better use of the land for those best fitted for the land.

The task can be helped by definite efforts to raise the values of agricultural products and with this the power to purchase the output of our cities.

It can be helped by preventing realistically the tragedy of the growing loss, through foreclosure, of our small homes and our farms.

It can be helped by insistence that the federal, state and local governments act forthwith on the demand that their cost be drastically reduced.

It can be helped by the unifying of relief activities which today are often scattered, uneconomical and unequal. It can be helped by national planning for and supervision of all forms of transportation and of communications and other utilities which have a definitely public character.

There are many ways in which it can be helped, but it can never be helped merely by talking about it. We must act, and act quickly.

From: Franklin Delano Roosevelt's First Inaugural Address, March 4, 1933.

Labor Unions Play a Part

The role of unions in America has almost come full circle in the twentieth century. Through the 1920s, relatively few workers were unionized. In most industries, management worked hard to keep unions out. Bosses didn't hesitate to fire workers they suspected of trying to bring a union into a plant. When workers did organize, their strikes were often broken by force. More often than not, when the police were called or matters ended up in court, the law sided with management.

Factory owners also tried to keep the unions out by giving their workers a few benefits. Owners spoke of their employees as part of their "family." They said they took a personal interest in the workers' well-being.

The hard times brought on by the Depression of the 1930s changed all this. Mass firings and wage cuts for those keeping their jobs ended any ideas about "family." Unions now seemed like a realistic answer to many of labor's problems. But power—and the law—still lay on the bosses' side.

Power began to shift through a series of confrontations between labor and management. Strikes, many of them bloody, began to break out across the nation. But now public opinion was shifting toward labor. Everyone was feeling the Depression, and people were less likely to sympathize with the bosses, though they might have during the good times of the 1920s.

Government also swung over toward labor's side. This was more than a matter of which side was right.

Unless workers got decent salaries and had some job security, the economy would never pick up. People needed to have money in their pockets and not be afraid to spend it. In the end, jobs and spending would benefit business as much as labor.

The Wagner Act, which became law on July 5, 1935, protected workers when they sought to form unions. The Wagner Act was named for Senator Robert Wagner who was responsible for introducing this legislation. The act also required that management bargain honestly with unions.

But building unions still required effort. Workers still had to apply pressure to get management to give in to their needs. In Flint, Michigan, at the end of 1936, that pressure took an unusual form. The United Auto Workers were locked in a struggle with the giant car manufacturer, General Motors. Instead of going out on strike, the workers stayed in and occupied the factory for forty-four days until the issues were resolved.

This "sit-down" action caught the imagination of much of the country. As Bob Stinson, one of those who took part, points out in the following selection, the workers were careful not to damage anything. These union members really were like family, looking out for each other. Many on the outside helped them too, sending in food and other necessities. It worked: the union won.

Today, after many years of prosperity followed by stiff competition from abroad, union membership is down. The reputation of American-made products has suffered in recent years and partly as a result, public opinion has turned against unions again. In the 1930s, however, unions played a key role in helping the country pull through one of its worst crises ever.

Recollections of a 1930s Autoworker

The Flint sit-down happened Christmas Eve, 1936. I was in Detroit, playing Santa Claus to a couple of small nieces and nephews. When I came back, the second shift* had pulled the plant. It took about five minutes to shut the line down. The foreman was pretty well astonished.

The boys pulled the switches and asked all the women who was in Cut-and-Sew to go home. They informed the supervisors they could stay, if they stayed in their office. They told the plant police they could do their job as long as they didn't interfere with the workers.

We had guys patrol the plant, see that nobody got involved in anything they shouldn't. If anybody got careless with company property—such as sitting on an automobile cushion without putting burlap over it—he was talked to. You couldn't paint a sign on the wall or anything like that. You used bare springs for a bed. 'Cause if you slept on a finished cushion, it was no longer a new cushion.

Governor Murphy said he hoped to God he would never have to use National Guard against people. But if there was damage to property, he would do so. This was right down our alley, be-cause we invited him to the plant to see how well we were taking care of the place.

They'd assign roles to you. When some of the guys at headquarters wanted to tell some of the guys in the plant what was cookin', I carried the message. I was a scavenger, too.

The merchants cooperated. There'd be apples, bushels of potatoes, crates of oranges that was beginnin' to spoil. Some of our members were also little farmers, they come up with a couple of baskets of junk.

The soup kitchen was outside the plant. The women handled all the cooking, outside of one chef who came from New York. He had anywhere from ten to twenty women washing dishes and peeling potatoes in the strike kitchen. Mostly stews, pretty good meals. They were put in containers and hoisted up through the window. The boys in there had their own plates and cups and saucers.

Morale was very high at the time. It started out kinda ugly because the guys were afraid they put their foot in it and all they was gonna do is lose their jobs. But as time went on, they begin to realize they could win this darn thing, 'cause we had a lot of outside people comin' in showin' their sympathy.

Time after time, people would come driving by the plant slowly. They might pull up at the curb and roll down the window and say, "How you guys doin'?" Our guys would be lookin' out the windows, they'd be singin' songs and hollerin'. Just generally keeping themselves alive.

Nationally known people contributed to our strike fund. Mrs. Roosevelt for one. We even had a member of Parliament come from England and address us.

There were a half a dozen false starts at settlement. Finally, we got the word: THE THING IS SETTLED. My God, you had to send about three people, one right after the other, down to some of those plants because the guys didn't believe it.

Finally, when they did get it, they marched out of the plants with the flag flyin' and all that stuff.

You'd see some guys comin' out of there with whiskers as long as Santa Claus. They made a rule they wasn't gonna shave until the strike was over. Oh, it was just like—you've gone through the Armistice delirium, haven't you? Everybody was runnin' around shaking everybody by the hand, sayin', "Jesus, you look strange, you got a beard on you now." Women kissin' their husbands. There was a lotta drunks on the streets that night.

*Editor's Note: The shift from 4:30 P.M. to 12:30 A.M.

From: *Hard Times,* by Studs Terkel (New York: Pantheon, 1970). Reprinted by permission.

Struggle in the Heartland

The following excerpt seems to describe a society gone mad. In the early 1930s, in a world where there were many children who went to bed without supper, farmers were dumping food in the road. Why?

The reason was overproduction. American farmers had been too efficient. They had produced such big harvests that the price of their crops dropped to very low levels. In many cases, these farmers couldn't even cover their costs, much less make a profit. They faced ruin if they couldn't make enough to pay the mortgage payments on their farm. Farmers were desperate, and desperation causes strange behavior.

Farmers often could not meet those mortgage payments. Banks foreclosed, seizing farms and putting them up for auction. In many communities there was such bitterness at this that the friends of a farmer would attend the auction, bid $1 for the farm, and threaten anyone who dared to place a higher bid. Then they would hand the place back to the farmer who had lost it to the bank.

By the mid-1930s, parts of the Midwest faced even more hardship. Drought, one of the farmer's worst enemies, hit hard. Without water, topsoil turned to dust. Then came the howling storms that blew away that soil, giving this area its nickname, "Dust Bowl."

Something good did come of all this hardship, as farmer Oscar Heline notes in the following excerpt. People knew they had to work together to salvage

The hopelessness and despair of this mother and her family was captured in a series of famous Depression era photographs by Dorothea Lange in 1936 (*Library of Congress*).

what they could. As in the sit-down strike in Flint, a common struggle sometimes developed a greater sense of community among people.

An Iowa Farmer Recounts the Farm Crisis

The struggles people had to go through are almost unbelievable. A man lived all his life on a given farm, it was taken away from him. One after the other. After the foreclosure, they got a deficiency judgment. Not only did he lose the farm, but it was impossible for him to get out of debt.

Grain was being burned. It was cheaper than coal. Corn was being burned. A county just east of here, they burned corn in their courthouse all winter. '32, '33. You couldn't hardly buy groceries for corn. It couldn't pay the transportation. In South Dakota, the county elevator listed corn as minus three cents. *Minus* three cents a bushel. If you wanted to sell 'em a bushel of corn, you had to bring in three cents. They couldn't afford to handle it. Just think what happens when you can't get out from under. . . .

We had lots of trouble on the highway. People were determined to withhold produce from the market—livestock, cream, butter, eggs, what not. If they would dump the produce, they would force the market to a higher level. The farmers would man the highways, and cream cans were emptied in ditches and eggs dumped out. They burned the trestle bridge, so the trains wouldn't be able to haul grain. Conservatives don't like this kind of rebel attitude and aren't very sympathetic. But something had to be done.

Some of the farmers with teams of horses, sometimes in trucks, tried to get through. He was trying to feed his family, trying to trade a few dozen eggs and a few pounds of cream for some groceries to feed his babies. He was desperate, too. One group tried to sell so they could live and the other group tried to keep you from selling so they could live.

The farmer is a pretty independent individual. He wants to be a conservative individual. He wants to be an honorable individual. He wants to pay his debts. But it was hard. The rank-and-file people of this state—who were brought up as conservatives, which most of us were—would never act like this. Except in desperation.

The hard times put farmer's families closer together. My wife was working for the county Farm Bureau. We had lessons in home economics, how to make underwear out of gunny sacks, out of flour sacks. It was cooperative labor. So some good things came out of this. Sympathy toward one another was manifest. There were personal values as well as terrible hardships.

From: *Hard Times*, by Studs Terkel (New York: Pantheon, 1970). Reprinted by permission.

The government, under the New Deal, became much more involved with farm life, as it did with labor. President Roosevelt pushed through a subsidy program that helped to avoid over-production by paying farmers not to plant too much. Later, many people criticized this program as too expensive, saying the policy favored the big farmers and unnecessarily increased the size of the government. At the time, however, paying these subsidies helped.

Roosevelt's New Deal government also became involved with the environmental problems that had created the Dust Bowl. It set up programs to encourage better irrigation and the conservation of valuable soil. In the South, this was combined with the production of cheap electricity in the Tennessee Valley Authority project, better known as the TVA. The TVA built nine major dams that produced hydroelectric power while controlling floods. Throughout the 1930s, Roosevelt's New Deal government would continue to expand its reach. Nearly every aspect of life was affected by the administration's new programs. This growth and increased control transformed the nation and forever changed the way government operated in America.

FROM BLACK NATIONALISM TO ROOSEVELT'S NEW DEAL: 1914–1940

1914

Marcus Garvey creates the Universal Negro Improvement Association to help African Americans live and survive without whites.

1914–1917

War rages in Europe. The United States joins eleven allies in the fight.

1917–1918

Revolution shakes Russia. The Espionage and Sedition Acts are passed in the United States.

1919

The Treaty of Versailles is signed. World War I formally ends.

1920–1929

Prohibition makes alcohol illegal. The growth and popularity of cars, radios, frozen foods, urban dwellings, and the rise of the middle class modernize America.

1929

The stock market crashes. Many savings and fortunes are lost within a span of hours.

1933

Franklin Roosevelt's inaugural address tells the troubled nation the only thing to fear is fear itself.

1935–1936

The Wagner Act is passed to protect workers who join unions. In Flint, Michigan, the United Auto Workers occupy a General Motors factory for forty-four days.

1933–1940

President Roosevelt's New Deal creates programs that involve the government in almost every aspect of the American economy.

FOR FURTHER READING

Berke, Art. *Babe Ruth: The Best There Ever Was*. New York: Watts, 1988.

Devaney, John. *Franklin Delano Roosevelt, President*. New York: Walker & Co., 1987.

Israel, Fred L. *The Federal Bureau of Investigation*. New York: Chelsea House, 1986.

Lawler, Mary. *Marcus Garvey*. New York: Chelsea House, 1988.

Migneco, Ronald and Biel, Timothy L. *The Crash of 1929*. San Diego: Lucent Books, 1989.

Polikof, Barbara G. *Herbert C. Hoover: Thirty-First President of the United States*. Ada, Oklahoma: Garrett Educational Corp., 1990.

Randolph, Sallie. *Woodrow Wilson*. New York: Walker & Co., 1992.

Stanley, Jerry. *Children of the Dustbowl*. New York: Crown Books for Young Readers, 1992.

Stein, R. Conrad. *The Story of the Great Depression*. Chicago: Childrens, 1985.

Stewart, Gail. *World War One*. San Diego: Lucent Books, 1991.

INDEX